a year in the life of yorkshire's three peaks

a year in the life of yorkshire's three peaks

andy stansfield

FRANCES LINCOLN LIMITED
PUBLISHERS

Frances Lincoln Limited
4 Torriano Mews
Torriano Avenue
London NW5 2RZ
www.franceslincoln.com

First Frances Lincoln edition 2009

A catalogue record for this book is available from the British Library.

9780711228542

Printed and bound in Singapore

1 2 3 4 5 6 7 8 9

To my daughter Grace and son Stewart in the earnest hope that the Three Peaks landscape remains as alluring for them as it has been for me.

contents

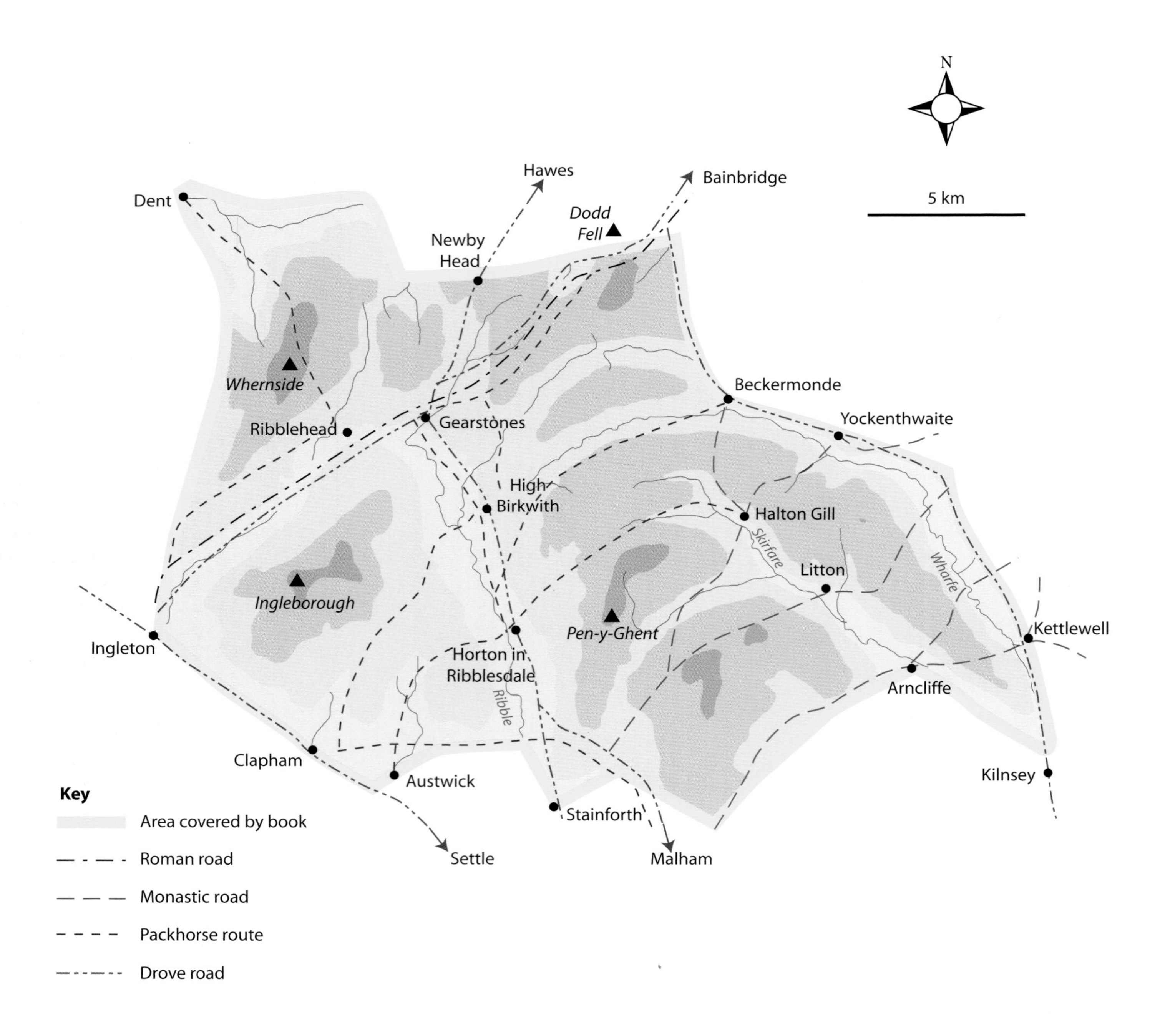

N
5 km
Hawes
Bainbridge
Dent
Dodd Fell
Newby Head
Whernside
Ribblehead
Gearstones
Beckermonde
Yockenthwaite
High Birkwith
Halton Gill
Skirfare
Wharfe
Litton
Ingleborough
Pen-y-Ghent
Kettlewell
Ingleton
Horton in Ribblesdale
Ribble
Arncliffe
Clapham
Austwick
Kilnsey
Stainforth
Settle
Malham
Key
Area covered by book
Roman road
Monastic road
Packhorse route
Drove road

introduction

The process of producing a book – actually the combined processes of capturing images, collating information, visiting the location, and pulling together one's own thoughts and feelings about an area – always springs a few surprises and in a way is a journey in itself. This one has been no exception.

Having lived relatively near the Dales for more years than I care to remember, I thought I knew the area well. But when you start to view locations through the camera lens with a very specific purpose in mind it is like using a fresh pair of eyes. You see things that you missed when you were simply out walking and photographing scenes in passing; particular subjects are viewed in a different context and take on a different degree of importance.

You also actively seek out places which would otherwise be off-route and therefore ignored. There are several specific examples of this in the pages which follow. Perhaps the most enjoyable discovery was the packhorse bridge over Thorn's Gill which, though I had read about it, I had never seen before. The same is true of some of the ancient tracks I had not explored previously. The business of gathering images also means visiting locations at times of the day which are different from the hour when I might normally encounter a scene in the middle of a day's walk. It also brings different memories associated with specific locations: that's where I lost a lens cap, leaning over a fence to photograph Pecca Falls. That's where I irreparably damaged a tripod when I dropped it en route to Gaping Gill, making the intended winch shot down into the main chamber almost impossible.

But there has also been the unmatched joy of introducing my partner, who had lived in Berkshire for 30 years, to the area and to a type of landscape with which she was totally unfamiliar. Having to explain to her how various limestone features come about, dredging up long forgotten images of A-Level geography textbooks in my mind, made me think about the subjects I was photographing far more than I would if I was working on a purely visual and intuitive level, which is normally how I work.

Throughout the year spanning these images, I often gave thanks for fine weather and cursed the Met Office in equal measure. The weather in this part of the world often differs significantly from that experienced on the coastal plain, just a few miles to the south and west where I live. I lost track of how often I left home in glorious sunshine to arrive at Ingleton or Horton in Ribblesdale an hour later in cloud and drizzle. All landscape photographers keep a close watch on what the weather is doing but not as close, perhaps, as the caving fraternity in this area. Sudden heavy downpours here can prove disastrous for those underground when water levels start to rise suddenly.

Water, of course, is the major influence here. The sediments which produced the rock were deposited in the shallow sea which once covered the area 300 million years ago. It was the ice of glaciers which sculpted the main features, but it was rainwater which continued to wear away at the bedding planes to create underground caverns and passages as well as dissolving exposed rock above ground to create the characteristic clints and grikes of the limestone pavements. So, instead of thinking that rain is spoiling your day out, give thanks for what it has created.

The area covered by this book is defined largely by the roads which encircle the Three Peaks area. The western boundary consists of the road from Ingleton through Kingsdale to Dent. Following Dentdale eastwards, the northern boundary follows the road up to Newby Head before cutting across country over Cam Fell then following the road through Langstrothdale to just north of Buckden. This arbitrary boundary continues down Wharfedale, branches off into Littondale then follows the road from Arncliffe to Stainforth, up to Helwith Bridge and past Wharfe to meet the A65 and back to Ingleton.

The area straddles the upper reaches of the River Ribble and displays classic geological features, including extensive limestone pavements, an impressive cave system, England's longest unbroken waterfall and Britain's second-largest cavern. The Pennine Way traverses the summit of Pen-y-Ghent while the Ribble Way follows the river from its source at the foot of Whernside. Steam trains still run through the area on the Settle-Carlisle railway over the impressive Ribblehead viaduct.

The whole area is criss-crossed by a network of ancient tracks which were previously drove roads, packhorse routes and monastic roads, most of which can still be followed today and are collectively known as green lanes.

The surrounding dales are equally full of character. To the east lies the broad, often-flooded Wharfedale, off which the tiny River Skirfare traces an intricate route through Littondale and the picturesque village of Arncliffe. To the north the equally delightful Langstrothdale runs west to east, surrounded by the medieval hunting domain of Langstrothdale Chase.

PREVIOUS PAGE: Thornton in Lonsdale marks the very south-western corner of the area covered by this book. Here the wall and trees of the churchyard frame an uninterrupted view of Ingleborough and gathering storm clouds, with the deciduous woodland of Swilla Glen creeping into the middle distance from the right.

ABOVE: Footpaths are plentiful and well-signed throughout the area, this one linking Kingsdale with Twisleton Scar End, a classic limestone scar with a natural cleft through which passes the old drove road of Craven Old Way.

ABOVE: Between Dent and Cowgill to its east, single-track roads run either side of the River Dee, marking the northern perimeter of the area covered by the book. The slopes of Whernside are seen here from the northern side of the valley.

OVERLEAF: The north-eastern boundary of the area covered by the book follows Langstrothdale westwards from Hubberholme, passing the National Trust's farming hamlet of Yockenthwaite. In the foreground the River Wharfe has carved a dramatic gorge through the limestone.

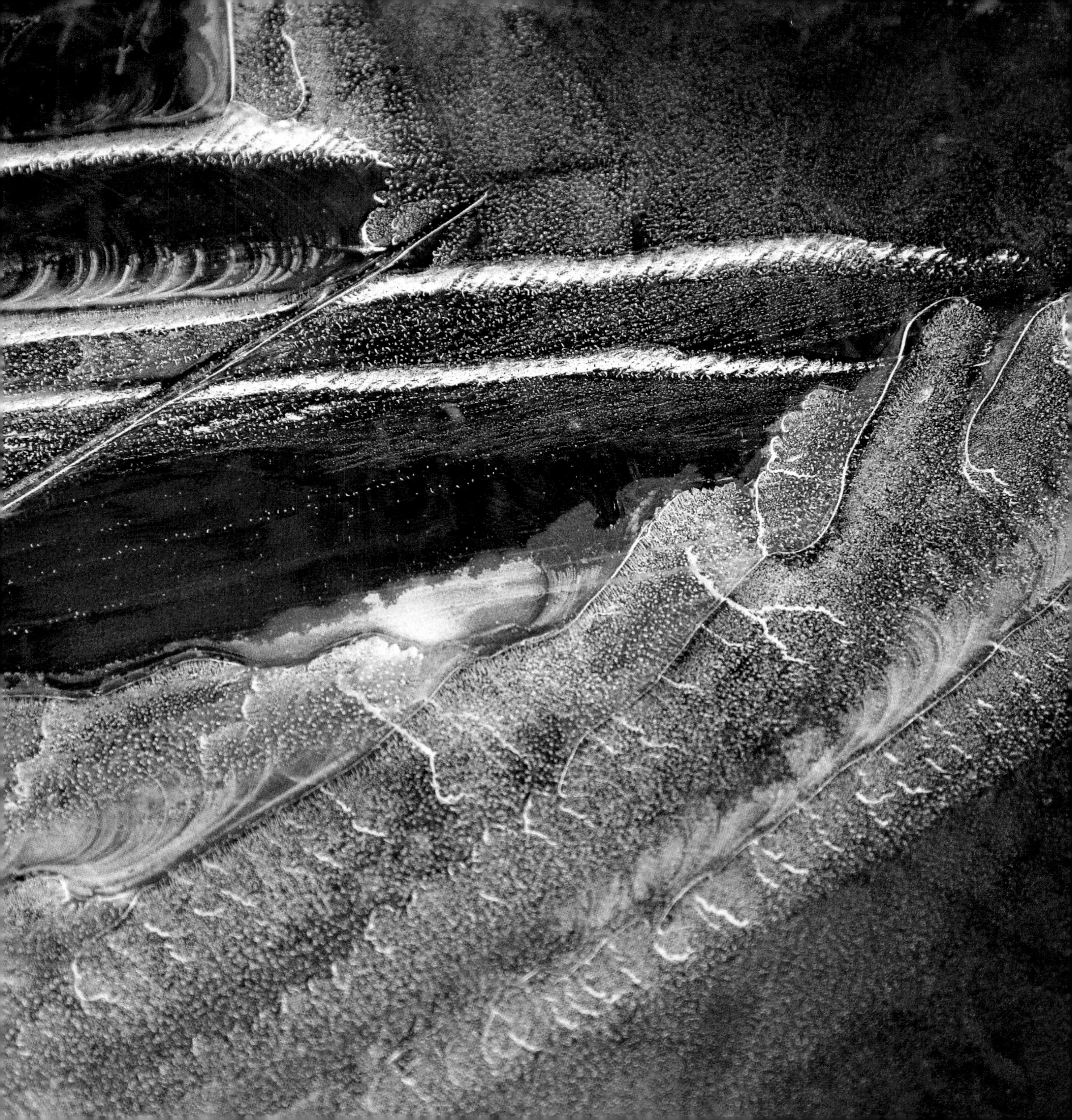

winter

This is the season when everything seems to arrive horizontally: rain, sleet and snow, wind and even the all-too-rare shafts of light from a watery sun, which rarely seems to climb much higher than the summits of Ingleborough and Pen-y-Ghent.

It is also a time when all ambitions are restricted to what is feasible on the day, walk routes are shortened, tasks are minimised, progress and growth is held in check, like the grass locked in by fanciful patterns of ice. Winter is for observation rather than effort, taking up precious moments of daylight to note how the ordinary becomes extraordinary in a landscape largely devoid of colour. Tiny details announce their brief importance in scenes we would pass by at other times of year, icicles and windblown snow and finally, as days begin to lengthen once more, the first shoots of green which herald the promise of spring.

PREVIOUS PAGE: A frozen pool of water, covering the grasses beneath, is in part crystal clear yet with elaborate patterns, caused by the wind and different rates of freezing.

RIGHT: A bright winter's day with some blue sky and sunshine makes moorland walking a real joy. Scattered sheep are almost camouflaged against the snow but their tell-tale blue and red rumps can be discerned if you look more closely.

ABOVE: Farming is year-round activity which brings untold hardships up here on Newby Head Moss. At one time Newby Head Farm served as a drovers' inn, an alternative to the renowned drovers' inn and weekly market at Gearstones, just a couple of miles down the road.

RIGHT: Gayle Beck reflects the watery early afternoon sun, with Ingleborough rising hazily in the distance.

OPPOSITE PAGE: As the road drops from Newby Head down towards Dent, it is joined by the Dales Way, shortly after which Dent Head viaduct suddenly looms large on the right. Beneath the imposing arches which tower above the road, this packhorse bridge peeks out from behind one of the central arches.

LEFT: Pen-y-Ghent from the east with an area of limestone pavement in the foreground. After Horton in Ribblesdale, this is the second most popular starting point for climbing the peak, following the Pennine Way to the summit via Churn Milk Hole and Gavel Rigg.

ABOVE: Known as the Ribblehead Viaduct and crossing Batty Moss, this impressive 24-arch construction stands 104 feet/31m high and is a quarter of a mile long. It is said that so many lives were lost among the 2000 or so navvies who built it that the railway company met the costs of expanding the graveyard of St Leonard's Church at Chapel le Dale, where they were buried.

LEFT: No matter what the season, cyclists traditionally take in a tea room or two during a day's ride, but in winter a good strong brew is especially welcome. Blindbeck Tearoom can be found just north of Horton in Ribblesdale.

The Pennine Way passes through this gateway en route to the summit of Pen-y-Ghent, whose distinctive outline is highlighted by a thin covering of snow.

Rain water has seeped through the rough moorland grasses, draining into a narrow stream. The air temperature was low enough to create these icicles without freezing the slow-moving stream.

Windblown snow clings to this gate leading to Rainscar Pasture, forming a distinctive pattern.

LEFT: Although there is little snow, the driving wind has compacted it on this wall end near Dale Head on the Pennine Way, south east of Pen-y-Ghent.

ABOVE: Just over half a mile south of Selside, this bridleway appears to lead directly westwards towards Ingleborough in the distance, but it soon veers south to Crummack Dale, with uninterrupted views of the second highest of the Three Peaks.

ABOVE: This moorland stream appears to lack a name on the 1:25,000 OS map, but is certainly pretty enough in winter to deserve one. The two huge slabs of rock bordering the stream indicate an ancient track crossing here, the flow of water being noticeably disturbed by the different rocks forming the stream bed.

RIGHT: At last, winter appears to be over and new shoots start to appear in this scene along the green road of Long Lane, which leads northwards from Clapham.

walking

In terms of numbers the most popular recreational activity in the area is undoubtedly walking, despite occasional major fell-running events such as the annual Three Peaks Race. Of all the various walking routes possible the single most popular choice is a 'straight up, straight down' tramp up Ingleborough, which is said to be climbed by some 130,000 visitors each year. Second to that is Pen-y-Ghent, though this is tackled through a mixture of direct and circular routes, plus a smattering of those completing the Pennine Way, which takes in its summit.

Although rail services exist through the area, the car remains the single most common means of arrival, so the frequency and location of car parks is an important factor in determining which locations receive the greatest volume of pedestrian traffic. Particular favourites are those car parks which provide additional facilities such as well-maintained public toilets and some sort of café nearby. Dent, Buckden, Kettlewell, Stainforth, Clapham and Ingleton all fall into this category but they are also all on the periphery of the area.

This leaves only Horton in Ribblesdale within the heart of the area and even then it is by no means central. But it offers a short route up Pen-y-Ghent, a direct route up Ingleborough which is almost as straight as an arrow, plus it is on both the Pennine Way and the Ribble Way, so short sections of these long distance routes are feasible too. It is also the base of choice for those tackling the arduous 24-mile circular route which takes in all of the Three Peaks.

PREVIOUS PAGE: *The insignificance of this lone figure relative to the dramatic cleft of Trow Gill, is especially striking as she negotiates the jumble of rocks which once formed the streambed. The rock face on the left has been extensively undercut by the passage of melt water at the end of the Ice Age.*

LEFT: *Walkers enjoying the wide open spaces of a landscape littered with huge boulders left behind by a retreating glacier, which was also responsible for depositing the more dramatic ones on Norber.*

BELOW: *After the fees charged by local council car parks, it is refreshing to find such a relaxed attitude to parking. In a fell landscape which is largely unfenced or walled either side of the road, it also provides some small measure of financial compensation for the farmer, whose roadside land is habitually used by walkers as an unofficial car park.*

While Horton in Ribblesdale isn't particularly well served by bridleways, Clapham certainly is. This makes it equally popular with off-road cyclists and walkers as well as those who wish to follow the easy nature trail and take in Ingleborough Cave, or even to extend that via Gaping Gill to Ingleborough itself. Ingleton, of course, is the location of the immensely popular Waterfalls Walk. While there is no proper car park, toilets or café at Arncliffe, the village provides easy parking with access to both riverside walks and routes over the moors to west and east.

Once up on the moors, with their open aspect and lack of boundary fences or walls adjacent to the road, there are many spots where roadside parking is both feasible and permissible. One of these lies just east of Pen-y-Ghent, actually on the route of the Pennine Way, where you will find an honesty box built into a wall. It would be interesting to know how frequently this is used! Possibly the best and most spacious roadside parking spot lies at the T-junction at Ribblehead. Though the selection of routes from here is severely limited, it does include a relatively short ascent of Whernside by picking up the Craven Old Way near the viaduct.

Ribblehead is also the location of one of the stations on the Settle-Carlisle railway, which also serves Horton in Ribblesdale and Dent. The Dales Rail service is very much designed with walkers in mind and operates every Sunday between 18 May-29 June and 27 July-19 October (2008 timetable). Two trains operate in both directions allowing roughly six to eight hours walking in between arrival and departure. There are additional bus links from the stations to other places in the area, but seats are limited so priority is given to those who have booked on a guided walk. There is an extensive programme of these graded walks, organised by Lancashire Rail Ramblers, which are led by volunteers from the Ramblers' Association.

The Ingleton Waterfalls Walk is a popular route, with parking and toilet facilities at its start. This couple are approaching one of the more dramatic sections which is fenced off to prevent accidents. A series of five waterfalls drop 100 feet/30m over beds of sandstone and shale.

Negotiating this stile over a dry-stone wall, this couple are enjoying one of those crisp clear days which follow the passage of a weather front, bringing the vivid blue skies which make everything seem so perfect. Generally speaking, 'through' stiles like this or ladder stiles predominate in the area.

Guided walks are sometimes looked down upon, especially by those who favour solitude or those who are proud of their map and compass skills. But they aren't just about letting someone else do the navigating: walk leaders are generally people who are steeped in local knowledge and their breadth and depth of understanding can add layer upon layer of additional enjoyment. There are also special interest walks run by organisations like the RSPB which can be immensely educational even if you aren't an ardent twitcher.

But the fact remains that the vast majority of people determine their own programme for the day and, if following a route for the first time, will come up against unforeseen obstacles and challenges as well as a few wonderful surprises. While the Three Peaks themselves are each a considerable height, much of the area isn't more than a few hundred feet above sea level, but its weather behaves like upland weather just about anywhere in the UK, and cloud and mist can drop to ground level in a matter of minutes. Route-finding too can spring occasional unwanted and sometimes unwarranted surprises, even in these heady days of vastly improved access to the countryside. The signs shown overleaf, demonstrate both welcome and deterrent in equal measure.

TOP: This fingerpost presents a dramatic picture against the vivid blue sky and the rocks of Nappa Scars.

SECOND TOP: It seems strange that someone, presumably the land-owner, should construct a stile where there is no right of way. Perhaps there was one, or at least a permissive footpath, at some point in the past. The map confirms that there is no access to the land surrounding Ingleborough Hall.

SECOND BOTTOM: The Three Peaks area has a long and well-established history as a focus for recreation, and walkers are generally welcomed. However, there are still occasional situations where access is denied.

BOTTOM: This footpath sign to Nelly Bridge in Dentdale has the unusual additional information that it is just one-eighth of a mile distant.

The dales themselves are generally well-served by rights of way in the valley bottoms, so choosing an easy low-level route, often with good riverside walking, is relatively simple. In some cases two dales lie parallel and quite close together, separated by a ridge which carries several paths – a good example being Littondale and Upper Wharfedale. This scenario can combine enjoyable valley-bottom walking in two different dales with a couple of upland stretches which provide fantastic views of both valleys.

For example, you can start from the car park at Buckden and follow the Corpse Road over to Litton, follow the banks of the River Skirfare to Arncliffe then take the bridleway over Old Cote Moor back into Wharfedale. Just before reaching Starbotton, pick up the Dales Way along the west bank of the Wharfe back to Buckden, a total of 11 miles and 2,336ft/712m of ascent. With a Youth Hhostel at Kettlewell and a good campsite at Arncliffe Cote, there is a choice of overnight accommodation nearby for good measure.

If you love limestone scenery and favour a day surrounded by the rock itself then the area west of the Ribble will be your choice. For those who prefer 'scar' country, the obvious selection would be the valley of the River Doe, running north west between the various falls north of Ingleton and Chapel-le-Dale.

On the northern side there is a bridleway parallel to Twisleton Scars which links to Chapel-le-Dale, from which you can follow the line of the Roman road back to Ingleton along a little used metalled road which provides excellent views of the scar from below. Alternatively, a more strenuous option on the southern side of the dale takes in Ingleborough itself and, east of Chapel-le-Dale, includes some excellent limestone pavement with trees growing through it. Both routes are between seven and eight miles in length, though the latter involves over 1800ft/548m of ascent compared with just 750ft/228m on the first.

For extensive limestone outcrops and occasional smaller scars -- provided you don't mind leaving the official rights of way and that you are competent with map and compass or GPS -- the area immediately west of the Ribble and south from Sulber Nick offers plenty of options. Avoid the south east corner of this area though, as it has been extensively quarried.

It is hard to understand why some people still insist on letting their dogs off the lead on land where sheep are grazing, but they do. This couple have the right idea.

There are many excellent guidebooks to the long distance routes through the Three Peaks area, often breaking the route down into daily sections which can be useful. But it is also worth watching out for those which include circular walks making partial use of these well-signposted routes.

To explore any of the above suggestions, or to devise routes of your own, the first thing you should do is to purchase the OS maps which cover the area. It is impossible to emphasise sufficiently how important it is in areas such as this that you work from 1:25,000 scale maps rather than the 1:50,000 series which provided a metric replacement for the old one-inch maps decades ago.

It isn't just a matter of scale and being easier to read: the 1:25,000 series includes one significant additional feature and that is the field boundary. The Three Peaks area contains hundreds of miles of drystone wall, every inch of which is included on these maps, making them invaluable when route-finding. Modern aids to navigation such the handheld GPS are useful, but should be used in conjunction with the map and particularly with your reading of the landscape itself. In short, they should complement landscape assessment and map reading skills, not replace them. On which note, don't rely on carrying a mobile phone for summoning assistance either, as coverage is intermittent in the area.

One fairly recent development for planning routes at home is the introduction of Memory Map software. With a few clicks of the mouse it is possible to plot an entire route in sections, instantly calculating time, distance and ascent. As a photographer I use the 3D facility to 'fly' along the route which gives me a good indication of viewpoints and the shape of the horizon. It is possible to print out the area of the map which includes your designated route – but I repeat the earlier caution about dispensing with OS maps. If the print out of your map is largely confined to your route it is not possible to take bearings from distant features in order to calculate your position, as you would be able to do with a full-sized map.

ABOVE AND FAR RIGHT: The lower reaches of the four and a half mile long Waterfalls Walk from Ingleton are bordered by areas rich in plant and animal life, part of which is designated a Site of Special Scientific Interest. This particular section contains orchids from Kew Gardens.

RIGHT: Thornton Glen is an attractive and well-shaded spot on the River Twiss and is managed by the Woodland Trust.

Waterfalls are synonymous with limestone country and provide a spectacular sight, especially after heavy rain when the water is tinged with colour such as here at Pecca Falls. Amateur photographers often ask how we professionals achieve the soft effect shown here. The answer is to use a tripod and a very slow shutter speed.

LEFT: At first glance this track on the edge of Arncliffe looks to be no more than a farm track. Persevere with it, however, and it opens out into a splendid walled monastic road (see above) which leads to Malham and is known as the Monk's Trod. Whereas the road to Malham follows the distant valley on the right of this picture, the monastic track climbs above Yew Cogar Scar on the left and follows an upland route to Malham.

spring

Long awaited arrivals mark the new season: longer days, spring flowers and lambs, and that magical first fortnight of leaf growth when the trees exhibit a strangely warm tone of green, reminiscent of evening light. But leave the wooded valleys and gills until later, when light and warmth have had chance to filter down to the woodland floor.

Early spring is the time to explore meadows and pastures, moors and scars, and the wide open spaces which respond first to the warmth of stronger sunshine. Free from moisture, the crisp blue skies which follow the passing of a spring weather front literally add another dimension to the landscape. Best of all, unless you are fortunate enough to have retired, spring brings Easter and bank holiday weekends, the opportunity to plan longer routes and overnight stays with a welcome pint in the beer garden at the end of the day.

PREVIOUS PAGE: Spring has sprung, though there's not much bounce left in this old boot spotted on a cottage window sill and now recycled as a plant pot.

ABOVE: Daffodils brighten up the churchyard in Clapham, a village where a number of ancient tracks converge, not least because of the existence of the church.

ABOVE: This ancient packhorse bridge is made more attractive with a show of spring daffodils.

FOLLOWING PAGE: View across Dentdale from the village of Dent, with Aye Gill Pike and Ride Hill in the distance.

LEFT: Some would argue that Three Peaks country is as much about broad expanses of sky as about the landscape.

RIGHT: West of Cam Fell, the transition can be seen from lush green pasture with occasional clumps of rushes, through fields with more frequent rushes, to rough grassland in the distance. The large limestone boulders deposited in the foreground somehow seem alive, as if they are actually grazing. The drystone walls, however, are in a poor state of repair.

OPPOSOITE PAGE: Imges of fluffy white lambs are a bit of a cliché when it comes to illustrating spring, so these ewes and their white-socked lambs photographed on the outskirts of Austwick were a welcome sight. They are Zwartbles, a breed which originated in the Freisland region of Holland but had to be adopted by the Dutch Rare Breed Survival Trust. They have now become a fixture in the UK, with nearly 150 registered flocks.

LEFT: This flock of Swaledale sheep being moved from upland pastures down to their farm in Kingsdale appear to have a faulty Sat Nav system, indicating a shortcut which is proving difficult to negotiate.

The first few weeks of leaf growth produces some vivid greens, dramatically displayed here against a clear sky and the sharply etched rock faces of Trow Gill.

The view north eastwards towards Long Scar from the junction of two ancient tracks, Thwaite Lane and Crummack Lane. The farming hamlet of Wharfe can be seen in the distance on the right.

Spring lambs in the pastures below Robin Proctor's Scar, named after a Crummack Dale farmer who fell to his death here. According to the story, after an evening at a local inn he mistakenly climbed onto the wrong horse to make his way home on a particularly wet and windy night. His own horse would have known the way, but this one became lost and both horse and rider tumbled over the edge of the scar to their deaths.

ABOVE: Nature's compass: exposed shrubs and trees will invariably slant eastwards due to the prevailing winds.

RIGHT: The farming hamlet of Wharfe with White Stone behind. There is no public highway for the last half mile into Wharfe, but at least all three tracks which lead into it are bridleways.

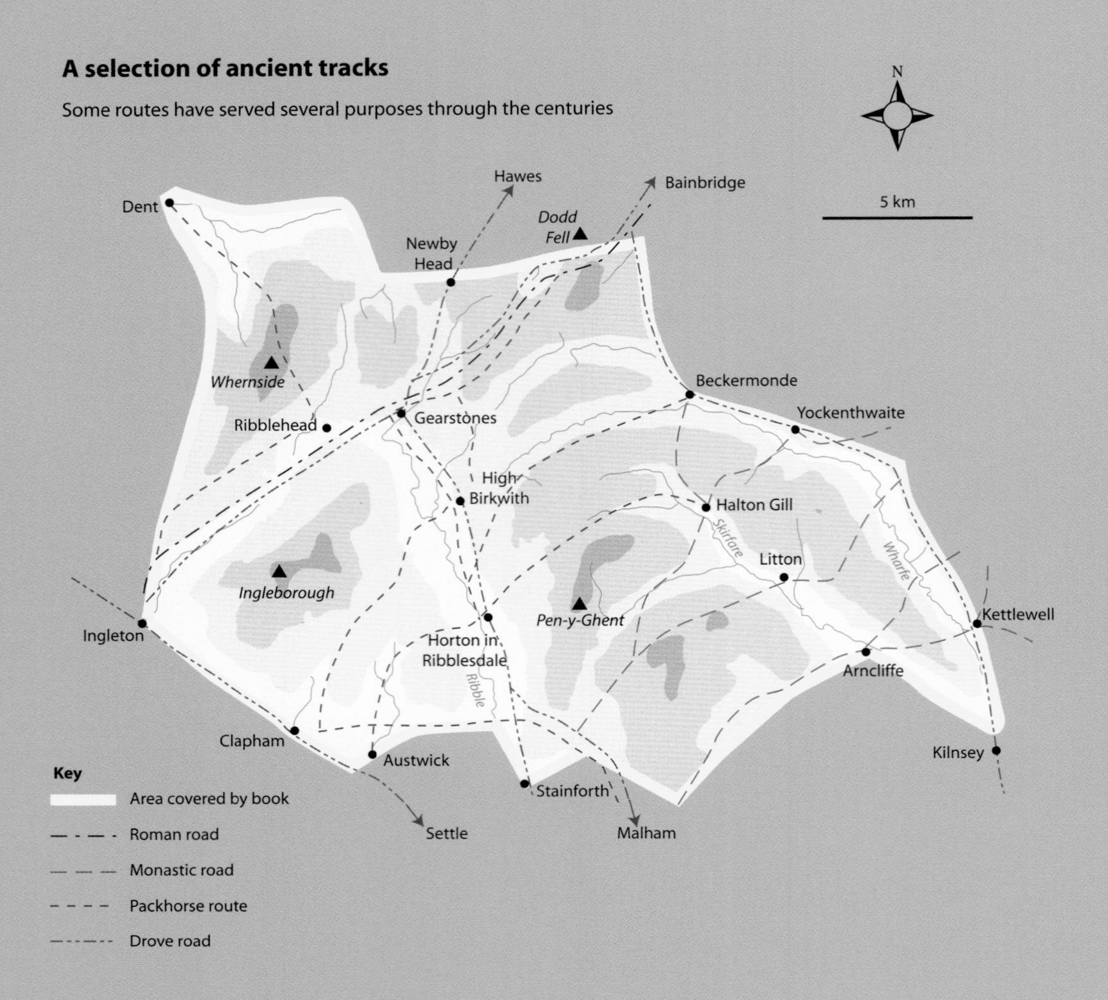

ancient tracks

The whole of the Three Peaks area is criss-crossed by a network of ancient tracks which were previously drove roads, packhorse routes and monastic roads, most of which can still be followed today and are often referred to as 'green lanes'. Together with footpaths, this extensive network of rights of way has led to the proliferation of recreational use over the years, as it is so easy to plot a circular route to suit every level of fitness and mode of travel.

Three unwelcome side-effects of this increase in recreational usage have been erosion, noise pollution from off-road vehicles using byways, and methods of travel which are inappropriate to certain rights of way such as cycling on footpaths.

The term 'right of way' is used to denote any path, track or road which crosses privately owned land and there are various designations, some of which have a basis in law and some which don't. The name 'green lane', for example, is a generic term usually reserved for ancient routes, stretches of which are indeed walled on both sides and look for all the world like a lane with a grassy surface rather than tarmac.

But the term has no legal foundation. These green lanes may or may not have rights of way running along them. Those which do may be designated as a byway open to all traffic, sometimes referred to by the acronym BOAT, or as a road used as a public path (RUPP). A relatively new classification, introduced in the Countryside and Rights of Way Act 2000, is that of restricted byway which permits travel on foot, on horseback, cycling and other modes of transport other than a mechanically propelled vehicle.

PREVIOUS PAGE: This ancient corpse road climbs Ackerley Moor out of Litton and leads over Haw Fell and Firth Fell before dropping down the slopes of Birks Fell into Buckden. Families of this stretch of Wharfedale had to carry their dead for burial at Arncliffe.

ABOVE LEFT: High Birkwith, now a working farm, once served as a drovers' inn on the route north to Hawes and Bainbridge.

ABOVE RIGHT: It isn't difficult to imagine this minor road from Horton in Ribblesdale to High Birkwith as a former drove road.

Footpaths as rights of way are simple enough in that they allow pedestrian use only. However, permissive paths (often wrongly referred to as permissive footpaths) are more complex in that the landowner can determine the restrictions which limit usage to certain modes of travel. For instance, he could allow cycling but not horse riding.

Bridleways permit pedestrian use, cycling and horse riding but not the use of horse-drawn vehicles. One of the problems faced by off-road cyclists and horse riders is that of bridleways suddenly being downgraded to footpath status – something which often seems to happen as the right of way encounters a change in land ownership or sometimes a parish boundary. A number of off-road cyclists have been known to ignore such niceties and also to use stretches of footpath linking two bridleways in order to complete their circular route, a tendency which has done the off-road cycling fraternity no favours at all in the eyes of walkers.

Less obvious, unless you know what to look for, are the routes which have always carried sufficient traffic to be continually upgraded and which nowadays form part of the road network. Clues as to their origins can sometimes be found in the form of milestones, tollbooth cottages and bridges which obviously pre-date the existing tarmacadam road, especially if the road had previously held turnpike status.

Concurrent with the development of turnpike roads, such as that which ran between Hawes and Lancaster via Ingleton, were the enclosure roads which were defined at the same time that previously common land was enclosed by Act of Parliament during the late eighteenth and early nineteenth centuries. Enclosures were often carried out on a parish or township basis which may go some way towards explaining the change in designation of some rights of way at parish boundaries, referred to earlier. Enclosure roads are often signified by long straight stretches with sudden ninety degree bends.

This unusual feature is the last thing you would expect to encounter when following one of the area's ancient tracks. You pass through it when leaving Clapham to take either Long Lane or Thwaite Lane, two of the area's best-known packhorse routes. In the early 1800s, the Farrer family gradually acquired all the land now surrounding Ingleborough Hall and extensively landscaped the area between the hall and the village church. Part of the landscaping project included this tunnel to carry the ancient right of way while maintaining the family's privacy, plus another tunnel which linked the hall's kitchen courtyard with the village, to allow the discreet delivery of supplies and arrival of servants working at the hall.

Packhorse bridges don't need to be wide because the combined bulk of the load and the animal's body are higher than the parapets. They just need to be wide enough for the person leading the train and the animal.

As a rule, roads develop for two main purposes: military expedience and commerce. This area was sparsely populated in pre-Roman times so neither of the above applied, with the possible exception of the route now followed by the A65 through Ingleton and Clapham which may have been used by traders in stone axe-heads and flint tools.

The earliest road of any significance through the area was that created by the Romans from Ingleton to Wensleydale, where it served the Roman fort at Bainbridge. Surprisingly the present day B6255, which initially follows roughly the same line north eastwards from Ingleton on the south side of the valley, doesn't meet up with the actual line of the Roman road for several miles. The Romans selected a route from Ingleton which carried their road along the north side of the valley beneath Twisleton Scars. The two different routes merge at Chapel le Dale with the route of the Roman road branching off over Cam Fell shortly after passing Ribble Head and Gearstones.

This short stretch has long been the hub of all sorts of traffic. Apart from the Romans who passed this way, this has been a packhorse route and the meeting point for two drove roads, as well as being an important road junction today for Dales residents and the setting for the Ribblehead viaduct on the Settle-Carlisle railway. Gearstones was once the setting for an important weekly market and drovers' inn, though it's nearly a century since a pint was last pulled there. Other former drovers' inns in the area can be found at Newby Head to the north of Gearstones and High Birkwith to the south, both now functioning as farms.

The routes used by drovers, although referred to as drove roads, rarely followed a distinct enough line to deserve the term 'road' and simply followed the valleys and gaps in the hills between them, covering a leisurely seven or eight miles a day depending on the terrain. This pace was an important consideration in an area which has few settlements, and one of the reasons that places like Gearstones became the site of regular markets in addition to those held in the few towns and villages in the area.

This fabulous packhorse bridge over Thorn's Gill near Ribble Head is my favourite. Spanning a miniature gorge 20 feet/6m below, it has no support other than the rocks either side of the gorge. The only man-made structure is the span itself – and even that looks perilously thin, with a single layer of hewn stone wedged into position.

Aside from the need to transport goods to and from local markets, which was the basis for the development of some packhorse routes, the Middle Ages brought another phenomenon to the Dales: the monastic route. Forget visions of cowled monks travelling the countryside to preach the gospel – in most cases these routes developed for reasons just as commercial as those which led to the packhorse routes serving the markets.

Huge tracts of land were owned by some of the more significant monasteries at this time, mostly granges which needed to transport their farming produce to their respective monasteries. The grange at Kilnsey, for example, transported wool to Fountains Abbey near Ripon, which also held land in Langstrothdale, at Horton in Ribblesdale and at High Birkwith. Packhorse routes like the Horsehead Pass, between Raisgill in Langstrothdale and Halton Gill near the head of Littondale, were used to carry the wool to the abbey too.

Over a period of time the monasteries developed other commercial interests and continued to expand the packhorse route network so they could transport commodities such as salt and lead. It is thought that the monks were probably responsible for constructing many of the packhorse bridges, of which there are some fine remaining examples in the area, such as that crossing Thorns Gill close to Ribble Head, though please note that it is no longer on a right of way..

The tracks which have their origins in the monastic land holdings in the area are, by and large, wider than those which evolved for use as packhorse routes.

There is another category of route which has religious origins and that is the corpse road. In rural areas it was not unknown for parishioners to walk many miles to church on a Sunday, especially during periods of history when attendance was enforced. This posed problems when funerals were necessary and the corpse needed to be carried several miles across country to the nearest church, a practice which brought about the term 'corpse road'. That is not to say that these routes hadn't been utilised for other purposes such as packhorses, but this distinctive use overshadowed all other terminology.

There is a classic corpse road from Wharfedale to Littondale, climbing southwards out of Buckden over Birks Fell before an alarmingly steep descent from Ackerley Moor down into Litton, from which the funeral procession would continue alongside the River Skirfare to the church at Arncliffe. That was a journey of over five miles involving 1300ft/400m of ascent while carrying the deceased, followed by another five miles home again which must have seemed a whole lot easier.

The village of Kettlewell lies beneath attractive woodland in Wharfedale. On the left of the picture, climbing the hill out of the village, is another classic walled green lane called Top Mere Road. This heads due north to join another track known as Starbotton Road, at which point alternatives branch out towards Coverdale and over Buckden Pike.

Craven Old Way is a splendid route from Dent to Ingleton, part of which is referred to on Ordnance Survey maps as the Great Wold, where it creeps over the shoulder of Whernside just below the tarns. It ignores the more obvious route from Dent to Ingleton via the steep climb up Deepdale and the sweep down into and along Kingsdale.

Instead, climbing the northern shoulder of Whernside, you reach the walled section called the Great Wold from which the views are staggering in every direction except to the south, being blocked by Whernside's summit. (Compare this with the climb up Deepdale whose steep valley sides restrict all views except northwards.) The route drops into Little Dale and the Settle-Carlisle railway just south of the tunnel under Blea Moor, then veers to the south west along another walled section above the Ribblehead viaduct.

The remainder of the route traverses some fine scenery and limestone pavement before dropping through Twisleton Scar End into Ingleton. This makes a substantial day's walk covering 12 miles with 1900ft/580m of ascent, always provided you can find transport from Ingleton back to Dent.

Today, the Pennine Way and the Pennine Bridleway make use extensive use of the some of these former drove roads and packhorse routes. They have the advantage of being both well documented and excellently signposted, making them an easy introduction to ancient tracks in the area, even if only tackled in short stages.

OPPOSITE: This monastic road leads from Foxup, just west of Halton Gill, around the north side of Plover Hill to Horton in Ribblesdale. The Pennine Way, shown here, follows the last section of it into Horton.

ABOVE: The Pennine Bridleway also makes extensive use of long-established routes, like this section from Austwick to Feizor.

RIGHT: *Thwaite Lane is one of the best known green lanes in the area, heading east from Clapham to Helwith Bridge. The latter half of the route now consists of a metalled road. Helwith Bridge and its crossing point on the River Wharfe was once the junction of several packhorse routes and drove roads.*

OPPOSITE: Crummack Lane can be seen winding its way over Norber Brow, with the extensively limestone pavements of Moughton beyond. The lane can be followed by car to just over the brow. when it becomes a bridleway.

Another popular starting point for exploring some of the area's ancient routes is Clapham, not least because it is easily accessed by road and has a large car park with toilets. It is a particular favourite of off-road cyclists because the ancient tracks which emanate from it are all designated as bridleways and several legitimate routes can be designed with varying degrees of difficulty.

The former packhorse route of Long Lane heads northwards, parallel to the footpath alongside Clapham Beck to Trow Gill but higher up the valley side. It is walled on both sides all the way to a point just east of Trow Gill before it opens out onto Long Scar, heading for Sulber Nick and dropping into Ribblesdale just south of Selside. From Long Scar another packhorse route, also a bridleway, drops southwards through Crummack to Austwick, passing the famous Norber erratics and crossing Thwaite Lane, another packhorse route leading east from Clapham, in the process.

Following any of these ancient tracks through this magnificent landscape, whatever their origins, is a pleasurable experience whether it is done on foot, by bike or on horseback, but there is also a distinct sense of being part of history which adds an unspoken additional quality to the day and makes it all the more worthwhile.

summer

With the sun now high in the sky, the dales and hillsides appear quite different. Water-courses are at their lowest, revealing sedimentary rock strata and small boulders carried downstream, varying in colour depending on their origin.

In early summer the flat emerald expanses of the flood plains of Ribblesdale and Wharfedale are vibrant during the middle of the day, while the ghylls and infant streams running down the hill-sides lack the sharp shadows caused by sunlight arriving at a lower angle. Instead, the varying shades of green from varieties of woodland, grasses and bracken are picked out, parcelled into enclosures by the white lines of limestone walls etched into the landscape. Whitewashed dwellings and farm buildings shine like beacons lighting the way home across a sea of green. And as summer progresses and hay meadows change their hue, a new range of softer warmer colours is added to nature's palette, accentuated by the soft light of dawn and early evening.

PREVIOUS PAGE: The fine glacial till and alluvium of Wharfedale's flood plain is responsible for the rich green fields, seen here at the entrance to Littondale.

ABOVE: First time visitors to the village of Dent are always taken aback by its narrow cobbled streets - and the fact that traffic can negotiate its way through the village at all.

Isolating wild flowers, such as these field scabious and harebells, against a background with a contrasting texture, always makes their colours and delicate structure so much more appealing.

PREVIOUS PAGE: Rise Hill rolls off the shoulder of Aye Gill Pike, the two combining to separate Dentdale from Garsdale to its north. Like many of the dales in the area, these have an east-west orientation.

OPPOSITE: A colourful mix of lady's bedstraw, field scabious and rest harrow brightens up this verge, the flowers basking in the heat reflected by the drystone wall behind them.

RIGHT: The significance of this image of Kingsdale Beck, no more than a trickle, lies in the date it was taken: June 26, 2007. Elsewhere in Yorkshire, the residents of Sheffield were trying to cope with flood waters up to six feet deep.

A late afternoon view across Ribblesdale towards Ingleborough, draped in low cloud in the far distance.

At seven o'clock in the morning on what promises to be a lovely day, low cloud still clings to Whernside, the sunlight just catching the Ribblehead Viaduct.

PREVIOUS PAGE: Arncliffe and Littondale viewed from the road over Nab End to Malham. In the middle distance, Cowside Beck performs some classic meanders while the high viewpoint clearly shows typical scar landscape on Yew Cogar Scar to the right.

LEFT: The brooding outline of Ingleborough stands high above the landscape to its west, with a small section of limestone pavement in the foreground.

By following the Clapdale Drive nature trail from the north end of Clapham, or the bridleway which runs parallel with it, to just beyond Ingleborough Cave, you come to this scene, a gate at the far end beckoning you into Trow Gill and towards Gaping Ghyll.

Viewed from the unusually-named Hesleden Bergh, the golden light of evening starts to cast long shadows down in Halton Gill and clearly delineates the gully formed by Halton Gill Beck behind it.

limestone features

The Three Peaks area contains some classic limestone scenery with extensive cave systems, limestone pavement, waterfalls and beautifully-sculpted summits like Pen-y-Ghent. Many of these provide opportunities for casual recreation with the added bonus of enjoying yourself while surrounded by magnificent scenery.

To fully appreciate the limestone landscape today we need to go back some 300 million years to its formation, as this accounts for half the story behind today's magnificent landscape. Rocks from the Carboniferous period are generally referred to as limestone, sandstone and shale but there are actually many categories of each, often named after the location in which they were first identified.

Typically, these rocks originated in a shallow marine or estuarine environment and contain the fossils of marine organisms such as brachiopods, corals and sea-lilies. These organisms sank to the seabed in huge quantities over millions of years and were ultimately compacted to form the sedimentary rocks we see today. But during this extensive period of formation conditions varied with changes to climate, water levels, sea temperature and so on. As a result the deposition of the sediments, and the compacting processes which followed, took place in phases. So instead of sedimentary rock being a single mass, it is actually laid down in successive strata.

The other half of the story behind the landscape concerns the extensive ice sheets which have covered much of the country at various times during the last two million years, finally dwindling northwards some 10,000 years ago as the climate warmed up. Wharfedale, for instance, displays all the hallmarks of extensive glaciation during this period, fed by a smaller glacier over what is now Langstrothdale. The glaciers not only scoured out valleys and ground down small rocks into deposits of till, they carried with them huge boulders which were left where they lay when the ice retreated. Some fine examples can be seen at Norber, where massive Silurian grit boulders perch precariously on smaller limestone rock outcrops.

PREVIOUS PAGE: *Smoothly-rounded hills, drystone walls and buildings constructed of limestone predominate in the area of the Three Peaks, as here in Dentdale.*

PREVIOUS PAGE: The Norber Erratics consist of a scattered collection of immense boulders left perched in apparently precarious positions by the last retreating ice sheet some 10,000 years ago.

RIGHT: God's Bridge is a natural feature consisting of a stream which has forced its way through the bedding planes of limestone strata, just north of High Birkwith.

Coupled with the fact that limestone is relatively soluble, you have an instant recipe for the 'karst' landscape we see today, as rainwater seeps through cracks and between the different strata. Further erosion from rain or rivers, and spray in waterfall locations, has affected varied rock strata in different ways because some are more soluble than others.

This has resulted in features which clearly show how water has permeated the rock and worked its way between the different layers, referred to as bedding planes. One of the most interesting examples is known as God's Bridge, just above High Birkwith. It isn't a bridge at all, but a section of limestone through which a stream has eventually forced its way between the strata, and over the top of which the footpath happens to pass. Although it is clearly marked on the OS map, thousands of walkers must have passed over this feature without even being aware of its existence. You have to step off route by 10 yards and climb down into the stream bed in order to see the way the stream has eroded the blocks of limestone, so it is best attempted in summer when water levels are low.

Above ground the pale grey rock has been eroded to create what are known locally as 'scars', which are outcrops where the soil has long since been washed away and the bedrock, itself well eroded, juts out dramatically and often exhibits scree-like rock litter at its base. Here and there, stunted hawthorns find root in the cracks and the rock debris has been used to create drystone walls and isolated barns. This is classic Dales scenery and areas which are devoid of woodland look equally lovely on a sunny day, be it summer or winter.

Exposed limestone can be identified on the OS map by use of the term 'scar'. The greater detail of 1:25,000 scale OS maps make them easier to use as they identify field boundaries, which in this area means mile after mile of drystone wall.

LEFT: Many of the Three Peak rivers and streams feature waterfalls somewhere along their course.

OPPOSITE RIGHT: One of the best places to study the various stages of waterfall development is along the Ingleton Waterfalls Walk, which includes Pecca Falls and Thornton Force, where groups of students can often be found on field trips.

Water has played a vitally important role in the landscape's formation and continues to provide good entertainment value today. Both the White Scar and Ingleborough Caves continue to draw in thousands of visitors each year to admire their respective oddities. Their caverns, passages and shafts are filled with a wide variety of cave architecture such as stalagmites, stalactites, curtains and flowstone, all formed by calcite formations. Deposits of calcite, a crystalline form of calcium carbonate, develop over a long period of time, typically growing by one inch every 500 years. Stalactites hang like icicles where drips of water form whereas stalagmites appear to grow upwards where these drips land. Unlike normal stalactites, 'straw' stalactites form as hollow tubes and flowstone, as the name suggests, is formed by water rippling over a smooth wide surface area. These features have been individually allocated such exotic names as Witch's Fingers and Devil's Tongue. Ingleborough Cave was formed from the outflow of the cave system of Gaping Gill which has one of the largest underground chambers in the UK, and is said to be large enough to swallow York Minster. Fell Beck drains into the main chamber, barely a trickle in the photograph above, and is Britain's longest unbroken waterfall, though the above-ground waterfalls tend to receive far more publicity. Twice a year the public have the opportunity to be winched down over 300ft/90m into the main chamber, on spring and August bank holiday weekends by the Bradford and Craven Pothole Clubs respectively. Also nearby is Hull Pot, which has one of the largest cave entrances in Britain.

ABOVE RIGHT: Gaping Gill (also spelled Ghyll) consists of a 300ft/91m pot which opens out into a huge chamber off which passages have been created by streams flowing underground along the bedding planes of the limestone. This image shows someone being winched down into the main chamber in a bosun's chair, next to the waterfall which has created this dramatic feature over the course of millions of years.

PREVIOUS PAGE: Limestone pavement consists of areas of exposed limestone divided into clints and grikes where mildly acidic rainwater has dissolved the limestone, such as here on the slopes of Ingleborough.

RIGHT: Clints and grikes in microcosm – even on this small scale the surface of a block of limestone shows how rainwater is beginning to work away at the rock.

One of the most dramatic of limestone features above ground can be found in the form of limestone pavements, of which there are numerous examples in this area, both on higher ground and sometimes down in the dales themselves, especially above Chapel le Dale.

Exposed limestone suffers weathering over long periods of time with mildly acidic rainwater gradually dissolving the rock. Eventually this leads to flat blocks of limestone which are divided into irregular blocks known as clints, the gaps between them being known as grikes. The same process can also be seen in microcosm on the surface of individual blocks of limestone where the early stages of erosion might only be a matter of millimetres in depth. More extensively weathered blocks often display a scooped appearance where small pools of water have gathered, dissolving the rock and creating some weird and wonderful shapes more typically seen alongside cascading waterfalls.

The ability of water to find its way downwards so easily through the surface layers of limestone has also led to the formation of swallow-holes or sink-holes where a stream has found its passage easier underground than above it. Very often the stream will reappear lower down the hillside when it meets a less permeable layer of rock – exactly what has happened with Gaping Gill and Ingleborough Cave.

Sometimes such large caverns are created that they cannot support their roof which then collapses. Perhaps the most dramatic example of this phenomenon can be found at Trow Gill at the head of Clapdale. This steep-sided gorge widens considerably, which must have placed enormous stress on the cavern roof prior to its collapse. Today the tree-lined gorge's vertical walls provide ample sport for climbers.

Limestone Scenery

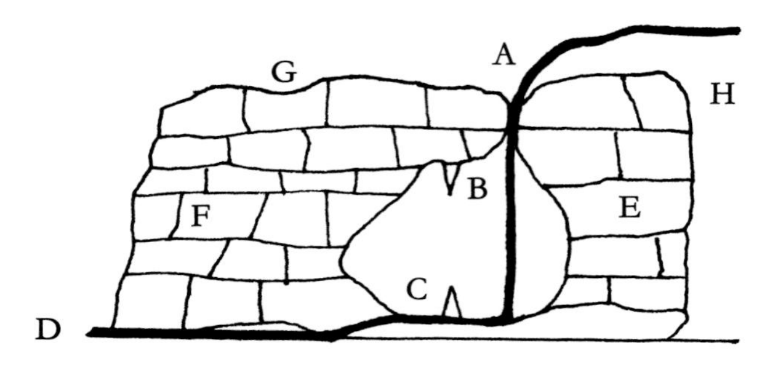

A - Swallow Hole
B - Stalactite
C - Stalagmite
D - Resurgence
E - Bedding Plane
F - Joint
G - Limestone Pavement
H - Impermeable Rock

PREVIOUS PAGE: This scene in Langstrothdale typifies all that is best about autumn in the Dales.

OPPOSITE PAGE: Woodland floors can be dark and wet and an ideal location for moss and fungi, a proliferation of which can be seen here growing on the saturated dead wood of a tree trunk.

ABOVE: For autumn hues Littondale is second only to Langstrothdale, both of which display the rich mixture of rust-coloured bracken on the hillsides and the rich greens and golds of trees beginning to turn.

PREVIOUS PAGE: The eastern end of Langstrothdale between Hubberholme and Yockenthwaite, with Rais Wood merging into Strans Wood behind the barn on the right of the picture.

ABOVE: The farming hamlet of Yockenthwaite, along with that of Cray plus nine individual farms in the Upper Wharfedale area, is owned by the National Trust. It is well-known for the Bronze Age hut circle situated in an attractive hillside location, just beyond the hamlet.

OPPOSITE PAGE: This garden in Arncliffe provided an interesting contrast between the shapes of the trees.

OPPOSITE PAGE: The view from Scar Gill across to Hawkswick Moor at the eastern end of Littondale, with the course of the River Skirfare marked by the trees in the valley bottom.

LEFT: The late afternoon sun picks out the rich colours of autumn leaves and the sparkle of Clapham Beck, as it passes beneath this silhouetted packhorse bridge in the centre of Clapham.

PREVIOUS PAGE: Ribbons of seasonal colour weave their way from left to right across this hillside, and back again; an autumnal gâteau with the limestone crest providing the frosting.

ABOVE: Facing west, the banks of the infant River Wharfe with a magnificent ash standing like a sentinel at the beginning of a stretch of the river which is one of the most favoured picnic spots in the area.

Facing east, the Wharfe traces its way between slabs of rock worn smooth over the millennia by the river in spate.

ABOVE: Autumnal colours etch these blades of grass against the contrasting wet rock, its strata buckled to the vertical.

LEFT: While last year's leaves still decorate the banks of Clapham Beck, this year's are starting to turn yellow and gold and a few have already fallen, drifting slowly downstream.

Index

Illustration captions in italics

Acknowledgements

Many thanks;
First and foremost to my partner Liz who had to put up with my sudden and unannounced departures, cradling my camera gear, when the weather changed, who continues to pass comment on my images and reads every word I write relentlessly, and whose support for my decision to become an author never fades.
To Outdoor Writers & Photographers Guild President, Roly Smith, who edited my text and whose command of the published word ensures my professional envy. To Sarah Slack who did such a fine job of interpreting my suggestions and designing this book.
For the passing companionship of all those I met in otherwise isolated locations. To the unnamed farmer who helped me to find the wonderful packhorse bridge over Thorn's Gill, the climber whose name I'm afraid I mislaid and who risked embarrassment while being photographed in Trow Gill, and whoever owns or previously owned the well-worn walking boots now serving gloriously as plant pots on a windowsill in Clapham. To Bradford Pothole Club for inviting me to their Gaping Ghyll 'winch meet', an altogether unforgettable experience, and to the count-less landowners I met whose informative and anecdotal background served to amuse, educate and enthrall in equal measure. To the Yorkshire Dales National Park and its officers. To Harry Penrice's Daily Outings On The Pennine Way, to Paul Hannon for his excellent 80 Dales Walks and Walks In The Western Dales, and especially to Geoffrey Wright for his definitive Roads And Trackways Of The Yorkshire Dales which enriched my walking pleasure beyond description. And, finally, to all those who appear in my images, unwittingly or by request.